I0829878

Black sand from a beach in Maui, Hawaii
Black sands and gold in sluicebox, Blue Ribbon Mine, Alaska

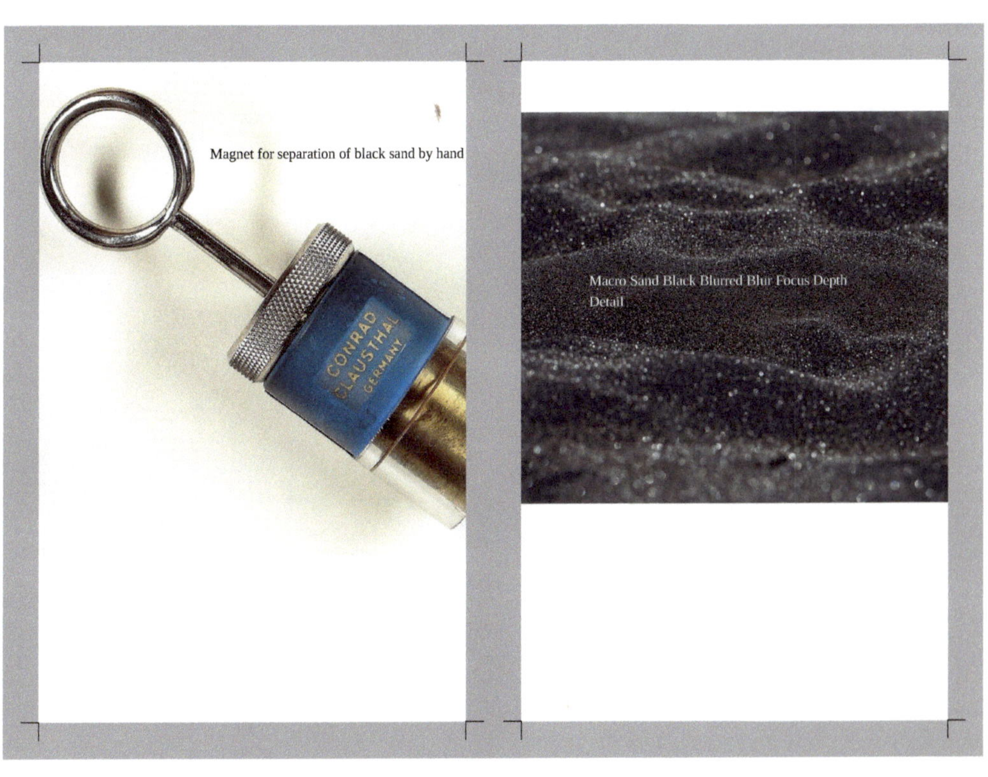

Magnet for separation of black sand by hand
CONRAD CLAUSTHAL GERMANY
Macro Sand Black Blurred Blur Focus Depth Detail

Beach Dry Crust Wild Waves Water Spray
Seashore Water Beach Ocean Sand Outdoors Summer

Black Sand Beach Pattern Texture
Black Sand Beach Hawaii Maui Beautiful

Water Sand Beach Sky Nature Landscape Sea Travel
Close-up of black sand

A green turtle basking on the beach
Sunset Waters Panorama Dawn Sky Nature Horizontal

Feet Mud Sand Volcano Earth Gatsch Black Tea
Black Headed Gulls Larus Ridibundus Waterfowl Beach

Sea Ocean Beach Black Sand Waves Coast Coastline
Iceland Beach Vik Black Sand

Sand Lienen Beach Coast Waters Sea Ocean
Water
Children and honu share the black-sand beach at Punaluʻu

The Henry Opukahaia Chapel

Boat Shore Fish Boat Sea Water Ocean Vessel

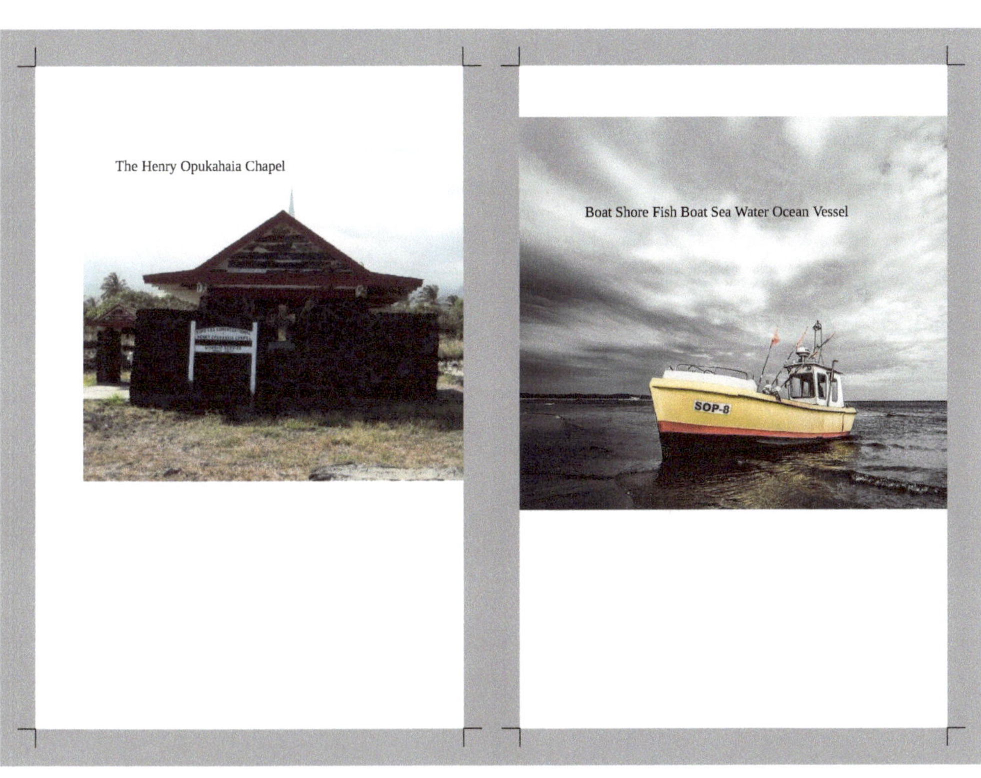

Sand Black Ilmenite Background Beach Texture
Nature Landscape Beach Seashore Rock Black Sand

Usa Beach Surfboard Wakeboard Surf Alone
Heart Sand Stone White Black Beach

Beach Volcanic Sand Sand Rock Black Summer
Sea Turtle Hawaii Black Sand Beach Ocean Turtle

Black Sand Beach Volcanic
Aircraft Crash Plane Crash Iceland Wreck Beach

Beach New Zealand Sea Coast Beautiful Beach Nature
Beach Palm Trees Hawai Sand Water Black And White

Sea Seascape Pebble Beach Coast Dawn Nature
Bali Ocean Indian Ocean Water Beach Black Sand

Turtle Beach Black Sand Sea Ocean Animal Nature

Coast Iceland Long Exposure Sea Beach Nature

Black Sand Beach Stone Tenerife Moist Seaside
Sand Desert Sand Dune Dune Beach Sahara Hill

Feet Black And White Sand Wave Bubbles
Nature
Iceland Black Sand Beach Ice

Yellowstone Lake Black Sand Sand Gravel Black
Sky Beach Black Rocks Sand Clouds Ocean Blue

Wedding Venues Beaches Canary Islands Landscape
Ocean Beach Black Rock Sand Island Mayotte

Beach Sea Boat Water Horizon Sand Black And
White

Beach Sand Black Dark Crab Animal Sea Ocean

Sand Sea Beach Black Water Stones
Sand Beach Stone Black White Foam Water

Water Black Sand Stones Beach Black Beach Sea
Beach Sand Ocean Sea Shore Rocks Landscape

Iceland Vik Beach Black Sand Cliffs
Spain Canary Island La Palma Beach Palm Sea

Bucket Scoop Baby Child Toy Sand
Forgetfulness
Vík Í Mýrdal Black Sand Beach Southern Iceland

Black Beach Black Sand Iceland Holiday Sea Sand
Yellowstone Black Sand Sand Gravel Black Volcanic

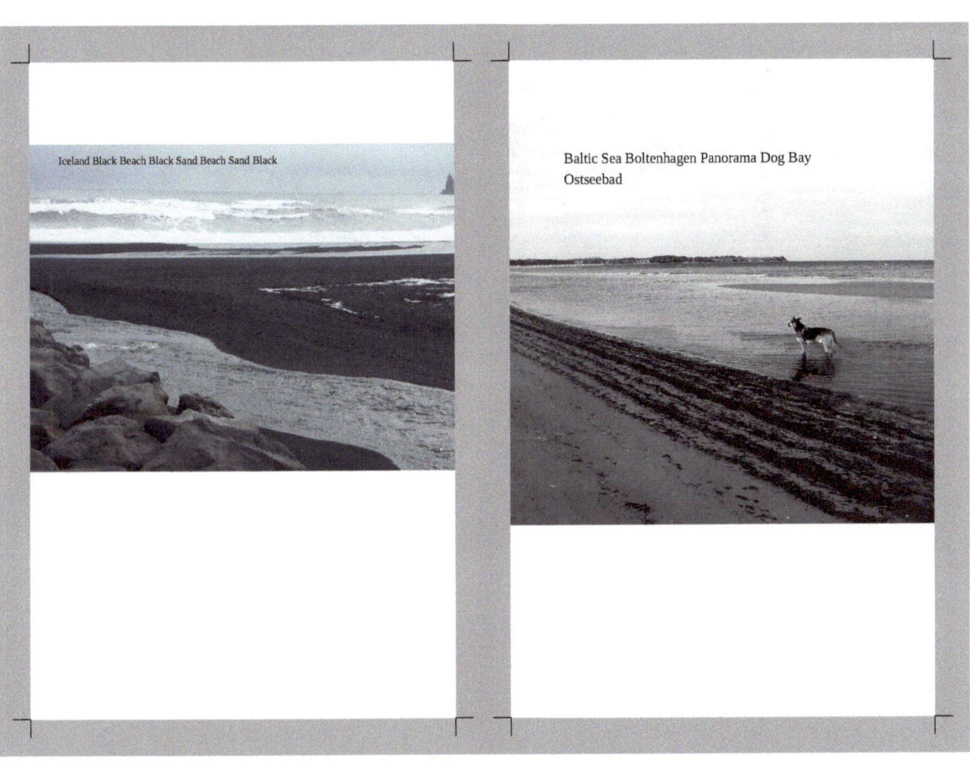

Iceland Black Beach Black Sand Beach Sand Black

Baltic Sea Boltenhagen Panorama Dog Bay
Ostseebad

Iceland Glacier Icebergs Black Sand Black Sand
Beach Bay Sand Black Sea Vacations Wave Surf

Iceland Black Sand Beach Icelandic Beach Vik
Big Island Hawaii Scenic Tropics Tropical

Beach Cliff Iceland Precipices Sea Black Sand
Black Beach Black Beach Sand Nature Iceland Stone

Ocean Surfer Black And White Beach Water Sport
Ice Transparent Beach Black Iceland Chunks Of Ice

Iceland Beach Sand Black Stone Rock Stones Lava
Beach Black Sand Rocks Canary Islands Palm

Flip Flops Beach Black Sand Seashore Seaside Coast
Sink Shell Black Sand Volcanic Sand Clam
Beach

Iceland Beach Black Sand Iceberg
Beach Deck Chair Sunbathing Sea Sand Black Sand

Beach Sea Water Blue Sand Black Sand Stone
The Sea Black Sand Beach Hawaii

Coral Beach The Meeting Black Sand Heart
Portrait Black And White Granada People Sand Beach

Sea Beach Italy Liguria Water Punta Corvo
Pebble Sand Stones Background Texture Beach

Beach Sea Sailing Boat Waves Sunset Water
Black Beach Ocean Summer Sea Sand Shore Iceland

Sand Pebble Stones Pebbles Beach Black Grey
Island Lanzarote Beach Holiday Mountains Summer

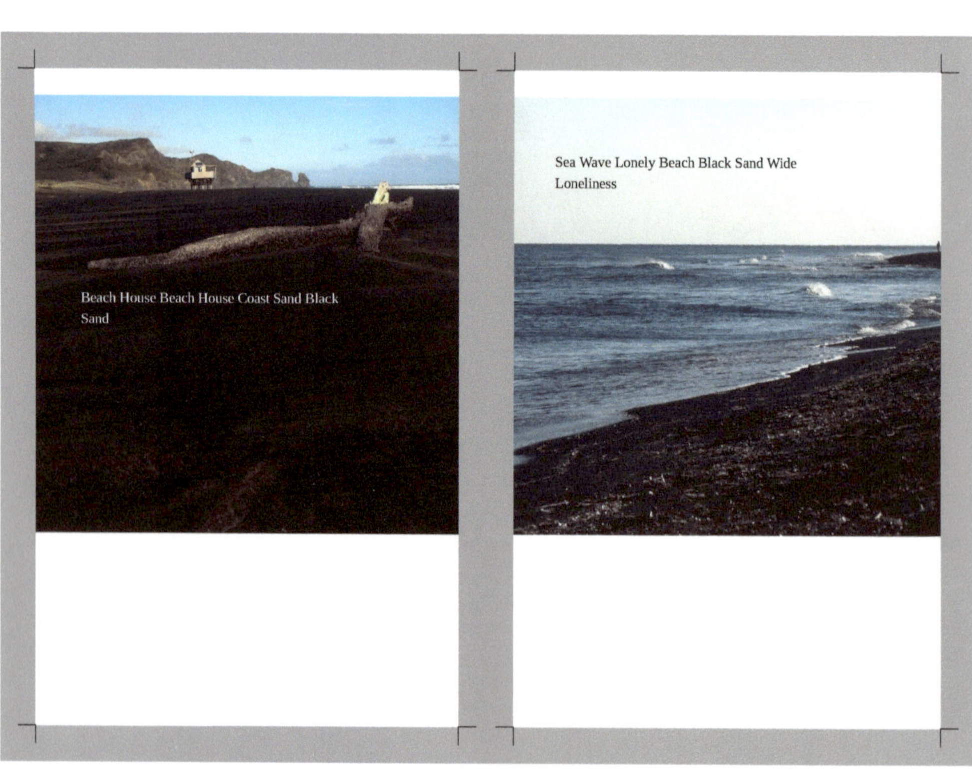

Beach House Beach House Coast Sand Black Sand
Sea Wave Lonely Beach Black Sand Wide Loneliness

Breeze Beach Sea Water Bubbles Tiny Waves Pebbles
Sunset on the coast of Ureki

Vík í Mýrdal from above
The cliffs by Vík, Iceland.

Playa de Martianez
The black-sand beach at Ajuy.

Punaluʻu Black Sand Beach Park

A photograph of the black sand on Kehena Beach

Black Sand Beach, also known as Kaimū Beach, Big Island of Hawaii, 195
Destroyed by volcanic eruption in 1990.

The distinctive salty black sand of Murawai Beach

Bethells Beach

Whatipu beach.

Sunset at Karioitahi Beach.

Proof

www.ingramcontent.com/pod-product-compliance
Lightning Source LLC
Chambersburg PA
CBHW040305240726
48664CB00006B/1380